A special gift for

_____

from

_____

GRANDPA, IS THERE A HEAVEN?

Katherine Bohlmann ❋ **Illustrations by David Erickson**

CONCORDIA PUBLISHING HOUSE • SAINT LOUIS

This edition published 2008 by Concordia Publishing House
3558 S. Jefferson Avenue, St. Louis, MO 63118-3968
1-800-325-3040 • www.cph.org

Manufactured in China
1 2 3 4 5 6 7 8 9 10   16 15 14 13 12 11 10 09 08 07

This book is dedicated to all the grandfathers of my family
who helped us learn God's Word:

Rev. Richard MacKain

Gerard Bohlmann

Carl Heitmeyer

Ervin Kimmel

Martin Bohlmann

"Grandpa, is there a heaven up so high—
A place to go when we will die?
Will I be lonely? Will I cry?
Is there a heaven up so high?"

"Yes, dear child, there really is—
A place of glory, peace, and bliss.
We will not cry when we are there,
Surrounded by God's love and care."

"Grandpa, Grandpa, how do you know?"

"Because the Bible tells me so."

*Never again will they hunger; never again
will they thirst. The sun will not beat upon them,
nor any scorching heat. … And God will wipe away
every tear from their eyes.*

Revelation 7:16–17

"Grandpa, death is very sad.
When I think of it, I feel bad.
Grandpa, is it all right to cry
When someone dear to us must die?"

"Yes, dear child, it really is.
Even Jesus Himself did this.
When His very good friend had died,
Jesus was sad and even cried."

"Grandpa, Grandpa, how do you know?"

"Because the Bible tells me so."

Jesus wept. John 11:35

"Grandpa, I know that Jesus died
And that His mother, Mary, cried.
But tell me, Grandpa, tell me why
Our dear Lord Jesus had to die."

"It was for you and me, dear one,
To take away the sins we've done.
All who believe and are baptized
Share Jesus' victory in God's eyes."

"Grandpa, Grandpa, how do you know?"

"Because the Bible tells me so."

*In [Jesus] we have redemption through
His blood, the forgiveness of sins, in accordance
with the riches of God's grace that He lavished
on us with all wisdom and understanding.*

Ephesians 1:7–8

Do you know, dear Grandpa mine,
Why Jesus was dead
    for such a short time?
Grandpa, why did Jesus rise
And then go up into the skies?"

"Jesus' work on earth was done.
And as our Savior, God's own Son,
He went to heaven to prepare
A place for us to join Him there."

"Grandpa, Grandpa, how do you know?"

"Because the Bible tells me so."

[Jesus said,] "In My Father's house are many rooms;
if it were not so, I would have told you. I am going there
to prepare a place for you. And if I go and prepare
a place for you, I will come back and take you to be
with Me that you also may be where I am."

John 14:2–3

"You know, Grandpa, I'm very sorry
When I've been mean
    or I've been naughty.
I know that Jesus must feel sad
To see me do things that are bad."

"He doesn't like your sins—that's true,
But Jesus loves and forgives *you*!
As you repent and trust Him, dear,
Even the angels rejoice and cheer."

"Grandpa, Grandpa, how do you know?"

"Because the Bible tells me so."

*[Jesus said,] "In the same way, I tell you,
there is rejoicing in the presence of the angels
of God over one sinner who repents."*

Luke 15:10

"Grandpa, Grandpa, is it true
That angels watch over me and you;
That when we're gone
    or when we're home,
They are with us—we're not alone?"

"Yes, dear child, our angels stay
At our side both night and day.
Wherever we go, they are there,
Protecting us with tender care."

"Grandpa, Grandpa, how do you know?"

"Because the Bible tells me so."

For [God] will command His angels
concerning you to guard you in all your ways.
Psalm 91:11

"Grandpa, now I think I see
All that you've been teaching me.
And when I wonder, I can look
In the Bible—it is God's book."

"But, dear child, how do you know?"

"Because the Bible tells me so."

*All Scripture is God-breathed and is useful for teaching ...
so that [those who have faith in Christ Jesus] may be thoroughly
equipped for every good work.* 2 Timothy 3:16–17